HOW TO USE A DREMEL FOR BEGINNERS

From Novice to Expert: The Roadmap to Dremel Proficiency

Michael K. Jumper

Copyright © 2024 by Michael K. Jumper

Table of Contents

Introduction to Dremel Tools

In the bustling town of Craftersville, nestled between the rolling hills of creativity and the vast sea of innovation, there lived a passionate yet overwhelmed DIY enthusiast named Jamie. Jamie had a dream—to transform their modest home into a wonderland of handcrafted decorations and bespoke furniture, breathing new life into forgotten corners and empty spaces. However, every time Jamie scrolled through online tutorials or flipped through glossy magazines, the complexity of the tools and techniques seemed daunting. That was until they discovered the magic of the Dremel tool, a revelation that came in the form of a book titled "How to Use a Dremel for Beginners."

The book was not just any ordinary guide; it was a gateway to endless possibilities. As Jamie turned each page, they were introduced to the Dremel tool—a versatile, compact, and powerful device capable of sanding, cutting, carving, polishing, and more. The book promised to take Jamie on a journey from a novice to a confident creator, equipped with the knowledge to tackle any project that sparked their imagination.

Chapter One: Unboxing the Potential revealed the history and evolution of Dremel tools, making Jamie appreciate the craftsmanship and innovation behind the device. It detailed the types of Dremel tools available, helping Jamie make an informed decision on which model best suited their aspirations.

Safety First, the second chapter, was a comprehensive guide on personal protective equipment (PPE), workspace safety, and common safety mistakes to avoid. This knowledge imbued Jamie with confidence, knowing they could pursue their projects without risking harm.

As Jamie progressed through the chapters, they learned about the different attachments and accessories, mastering techniques for sanding, cutting, engraving, and polishing. The book was meticulously structured, offering step-by-step instructions, detailed illustrations, and practical tips for setting up a workspace, choosing the right attachment for each project, and maintaining the tool to ensure longevity.

But what truly set this book apart were the Step-by-Step Beginner Projects. Jamie was thrilled to find projects that matched their skill level, each designed to build confidence and skill progressively. From personalizing wooden kitchen utensils to upcycling vintage frames, Jamie embarked on a creative journey, with the book as their trusted companion.

Troubleshooting common issues and advanced tips and tricks further enriched Jamie's learning experience. They discovered how to enhance precision in detailed work, mix mediums and materials, and even customize their Dremel tool for unique projects.

"Why should you buy this book?" Jamie mused, as they admired their newly crafted decorations and furniture, each piece a testament to their journey from a hesitant beginner to a skilled creator. The answer was simple: "How to Use a Dremel for Beginners" was more than just a guide; it was a mentor, a source of inspiration, and a companion on a journey of creativity and self-discovery.

For anyone standing at the threshold of their crafting journey, overwhelmed by the complexity of tools and techniques, this book promises to demystify the Dremel tool, guiding you through every step with clarity, patience, and expertise. Like Jamie, you'll soon transform your space with creations that reflect your unique vision, all while enjoying the fulfilling journey of bringing your ideas to life.

What is a Dremel Tool?

A Dremel tool is a versatile, handheld rotary device that has transformed the world of DIY projects, crafting, and home improvement. Known for its high speed, compact size, and incredible precision, it stands out as an essential tool for anyone looking to engage in detailed work or creative projects. The Dremel tool's unique selling point lies in its ability to perform a wide range of tasks with ease and efficiency, making it a must-have for beginners and seasoned crafters alike.

At the heart of a Dremel tool's functionality is its rotary motion, powered by a motor that allows the attachment or accessory at its tip to spin at high speeds. This fundamental mechanism enables it to cut, carve, engrave, sand, grind, polish, and clean different materials including wood, metal, glass, and plastic, among others. What makes the Dremel tool particularly appealing to beginners is its user-friendly design. The tool is lightweight, easy to handle, and allows for precise control, which is crucial when working on intricate designs or delicate materials.

The versatility of the Dremel tool is further enhanced by its wide array of attachments and accessories. Each attachment is designed for a specific task, ranging from cutting wheels and sanding bands to engraving bits and polishing pads. This interchangeable system not only expands the range of projects one can undertake but also ensures that tasks can be completed with a level of precision and finish that is difficult to achieve with more traditional tools.

For beginners, learning how to use a Dremel tool starts with understanding the importance of choosing the right attachment for the job. This decision is critical for both the success of the project and the longevity of the tool. Additionally, mastering the technique of changing attachments safely and efficiently is a foundational skill that enhances the user experience.

One of the most significant benefits of using a Dremel tool is its ability to empower individuals to tackle a variety of projects without the need for a vast collection of specialized tools. From personalizing wooden kitchen utensils to restoring antique furniture or crafting handmade jewelry, the possibilities are nearly endless. This multipurpose nature, combined with the tool's ease of use, makes it an ideal choice for beginners eager to explore their creativity and develop their skills.

Moreover, the Dremel tool is not just about the projects it can create; it's also about the learning journey it offers. Beginners will find that as they grow more comfortable with the tool, they can gradually take on more complex projects, experimenting with different materials and techniques. This progression not only enhances their crafting skills but also builds confidence in their ability to bring their visions to life.

The Dremel tool is much more than a simple rotary tool; it is a gateway to the world of crafting, DIY projects, and home improvement. Its compact size, versatility, and precision make it an indispensable tool for beginners, offering a hands-on learning experience that is both rewarding and fun. Whether one is looking to undertake their first project or explore new creative avenues, the Dremel tool provides the means to achieve impressive results with a personal touch.

History and Evolution of Dremel Tools

The story of Dremel tools begins in 1932, when Albert J. Dremel founded the Dremel Manufacturing Company in Racine, Wisconsin. An inventor by nature, Dremel sought to create a compact, versatile tool that would empower hobbyists and professionals alike. His vision led to the creation of the first Dremel rotary tool, a revolutionary piece of equipment that combined multiple functionalities into one lightweight, handheld device. This innovation allowed users to drill, grind, sand, and polish with a single tool, marking a significant advancement in the world of power tools.

Over the decades, Dremel tools have evolved significantly. The original model set the foundation for a line of rotary tools known for their reliability, durability, and precision. In the years following its inception, Dremel's company introduced various attachments and accessories, expanding the tool's versatility. These ranged from router attachments for woodworking to flex shafts for intricate jewelry making, enabling craftsmen to explore a broader array of projects with greater detail and accuracy.

The 1950s and 1960s saw further innovation with the introduction of cordless models, which offered users the freedom to work without the constraint of power cords. This development was particularly beneficial for outdoor projects or in spaces where electrical outlets were not readily available. The introduction of variable speed controls in later models allowed users to adjust the tool's speed to suit different materials and applications, enhancing precision and control.

Dremel's commitment to innovation was also evident in its educational initiatives. Recognizing that the potential of their tools extended as far as the user's skill and imagination, Dremel began producing instructional materials and guides. These resources aimed to inspire users with project ideas, teach new techniques, and ensure that even beginners could achieve professional-quality results with their Dremel tools.

The turn of the century brought digital advancements, and with it, Dremel adapted to the changing landscape by incorporating modern technologies into their tools. The company introduced high-performance models with improved motor designs, electronic feedback for consistent speed under load, and lithium-ion batteries for longer run times and enhanced portability.

Today, Dremel tools are synonymous with creativity and innovation. They are used by DIY enthusiasts, craftsmen, and professionals in a myriad of fields, including woodworking, metalworking, jewelry making, and even pumpkin carving. The brand has grown to include a wide range of tools beyond the rotary tool, such as oscillating multi-tools, benchtop devices like scroll saws, and even 3D printers, reflecting the company's commitment to innovation and quality.

The evolution of Dremel tools is a testament to the enduring vision of Albert J. Dremel. From a single rotary tool to a vast lineup of devices and accessories, Dremel has remained at the forefront of the power tool industry, empowering users to explore the limits of their creativity. For beginners, the rich history and evolution of Dremel tools underscore the importance of choosing versatile, high-quality tools that grow with their skills, enabling them to bring any project, no matter how ambitious, to life.

Types of Dremel Tools

Dremel tools, renowned for their versatility and ease of use, are a staple in the toolkit of hobbyists, DIY enthusiasts, and professionals alike. At the heart of their appeal is the wide range of models and attachments available, each designed to accommodate an array of tasks from intricate craft projects to robust home improvement jobs. Understanding the different types of Dremel tools is essential for beginners, as it helps in selecting the right tool for specific projects, ensuring both safety and efficiency.

The classic Dremel Rotary Tool is perhaps the most well-known in the Dremel lineup. These tools are distinguished by their fast-rotating bits, which can cut, carve, engrave, sand, grind, and polish various materials. The rotary tool's versatility is further enhanced by a comprehensive selection of attachments and accessories, making it a go-to solution for detailed work on wood, metal, glass, and more. Some models offer variable speed settings, allowing users to adjust the tool's speed based on the material they are working with and the precision required for the task.

For those interested in heavier-duty tasks, such as cutting through tile or metal, the Dremel Saw-Max might be the ideal choice. This compact, handheld saw allows for straight, plunge, and flush cuts, making it perfect for remodeling projects, like installing new flooring or cutting openings in walls. Its ergonomic design and precise control make it suitable for beginners who need a reliable tool for more demanding cuts.

Another notable type is the Dremel VersaTip, a butane soldering iron that excels in pyrography, soldering, and hot cutting. This tool is particularly appealing to crafters who work with metal or need an effective tool for detailed wood burning projects. Its portability, fueled by butane, ensures that it can be used anywhere, without the need for an electrical outlet.

For cleaning and polishing tasks, the Dremel Versa stands out. This power cleaner takes the elbow grease out of scrubbing, offering a high-speed cleaning tool that can tackle soap scum, oven grime, and even rust. With a variety of cleaning pads available, it's highly effective on different surfaces, from bathroom tiles to outdoor furniture, making it a valuable tool for keeping home and garden in pristine condition.

Lastly, the Dremel Lite is a cordless rotary tool designed for convenience and ease of use. Ideal for beginners, its lightweight design and simplicity make it perfect for a variety of projects, including crafting, engraving, and small repairs. Its cordless nature ensures flexibility and ease of movement, allowing users to work on projects anywhere, without being tethered to a power outlet.

Each Dremel tool type serves a specific purpose, yet all share the common qualities of versatility, reliability, and ease of use. For beginners, understanding these different types and their applications is the first step towards mastering Dremel tools and unleashing their creative potential. Whether it's crafting a piece of jewelry, renovating a piece of furniture, or undertaking a home improvement project, there's a Dremel tool that can make the process smoother, faster, and more enjoyable.

Overview of Dremel Tool Uses

The Dremel tool, a versatile and compact rotary tool, opens up a world of possibilities for both beginners and seasoned DIY enthusiasts. Designed to perform a multitude of tasks with precision and ease, its uses span from simple home improvement tasks to intricate crafting projects. One of the most appealing aspects of the Dremel tool is its adaptability to various materials, including wood, metal, glass, ceramics, and even plastic, making it an indispensable tool in any creator's arsenal.

For beginners, starting with sanding and polishing offers a gentle introduction to the capabilities of the Dremel tool. Sanding attachments can smooth rough edges on wooden furniture or carve shapes into wood crafts, while polishing accessories bring a high shine to metals and jewelry. This foundational knowledge serves as a stepping stone to more complex projects.

Cutting is another fundamental use, with specialized bits designed to cut through different materials. Whether it's crafting a custom shelving unit or adjusting the length of a copper pipe, the Dremel ensures precise and clean cuts. The ability to make intricate cuts also enables hobbyists to delve into detailed woodworking and metalworking projects, expanding their creative repertoire.

Engraving and etching with a Dremel tool are particularly popular among beginners for personalizing items. From glassware to metal keepsakes, the tool allows for the addition of detailed designs and text, making it perfect for creating gifts or unique home decor. The precision of the Dremel tool is unmatched, offering control over depth and detail that is difficult to achieve with other engraving tools.

Carving is another area where the Dremel tool excels. Whether it's carving intricate designs into wood, etching patterns into leather, or sculpting shapes out of soft metals, the Dremel's range of carving bits and attachments provides the versatility needed for various materials and textures.

Drilling with a Dremel tool is particularly useful for delicate tasks where precision is paramount. It is ideal for creating pilot holes, drilling small holes in jewelry beads, or even intricate woodworking where standard drills are too bulky and powerful.

The Dremel tool also shines in the realm of restoration and repair. It can be used to remove rust from metal objects, repair damaged furniture by sanding away imperfections, or even clean and restore antique items. Its precision and control make it an excellent tool for sensitive restoration projects that require a gentle touch.

For hobbyists interested in model building or crafting, the Dremel tool is invaluable. It can be used to shape model components, create textures, or modify parts with precision that hand tools cannot match. The tool's ability to work with a wide range of materials means that it can be used in virtually any aspect of model making.

Finally, the Dremel tool is an essential tool for DIY home improvement projects. From cutting tile for a backsplash to routing grooves for wiring, the Dremel tool's versatility makes it a go-to solution for intricate tasks that larger power tools cannot handle.

The Dremel tool is a multi-functional powerhouse that enables beginners to explore a wide array of projects across different materials. Its ease of use, combined with the extensive range of attachments and accessories, allows for endless creativity and precision in crafting, making it a fundamental tool for anyone interested in DIY projects, crafting, or home improvement.

Safety First: Understanding the Risks

Personal Protective Equipment (PPE)

Personal Protective Equipment (PPE) is crucial for ensuring safety while using a Dremel tool, especially for beginners unfamiliar with its operation. PPE helps mitigate risks associated with rotary tool use, such as flying debris, dust inhalation, and accidental contact with the tool bit. Understanding and properly utilizing PPE can greatly reduce the chances of injury during crafting, DIY projects, or home improvements.

Eye protection is paramount when working with a Dremel tool. Safety glasses or goggles shield the eyes from harmful dust particles, wood shavings, metal filings, and other debris that can cause serious eye injuries. For tasks that generate a significant amount of dust or flying particles, a face shield can offer additional protection, covering not just the eyes but the entire face.

Hearing protection should not be overlooked, especially during extended use of the Dremel tool or when working on projects that produce high levels of noise. Earplugs or earmuffs can protect against hearing damage, ensuring that hobbyists can enjoy their crafting endeavors for years to come without compromising their hearing health.

Respiratory protection is another critical aspect of PPE. Dust masks or respirators are essential when sanding, carving, or cutting materials that generate fine dust or harmful particles. A proper mask can prevent inhalation of wood dust, metal particles, or other irritants that can lead to respiratory issues.

Hand protection, such as gloves, is advisable to protect against cuts, abrasions, and burns. However, it's important to choose the right type of gloves for the task at hand. For precision work that requires a high degree of dexterity, thin, tight-fitting gloves offer protection without compromising control. For tasks that involve handling hot materials or sharp edges, thicker gloves may be necessary to provide adequate protection.

Proper attire plays a role in safety as well. Wearing long sleeves and pants can protect the skin from debris and sparks. Additionally, clothing should be snug-fitting to avoid getting caught in the rotating parts of the tool. Aprons or smocks made from durable materials can provide an extra layer of protection and keep clothes clean.

Footwear is also an important consideration. Closed-toe shoes made from durable materials protect the feet from falling objects, sharp debris, or accidental spills. For projects that involve heavy materials or where there is a risk of dropping the tool, safety shoes with reinforced toes can offer additional protection.

Lastly, maintaining a well-ventilated workspace is essential to ensure that any hazardous dust or fumes are effectively dispersed. For tasks that generate toxic fumes or significant dust, working in a well-ventilated area or using a dust extraction system can help maintain a safe breathing environment.

For beginners, understanding and implementing the correct use of Personal Protective Equipment is the first step towards safely enjoying the vast possibilities that a Dremel tool offers. It not only ensures personal safety but also enhances the overall experience by allowing users to focus on their creativity and projects without the worry of injury. Remember, safety is the foundation upon which all great DIY projects are built.

Workspace Safety

When embarking on projects with a Dremel tool, prioritizing workspace safety is essential. This compact yet powerful tool, while invaluable for a myriad of crafting, engraving, and DIY tasks, poses risks if proper safety measures are not observed. Ensuring a safe working environment not only protects the user but also enhances the efficiency and quality of the work being undertaken.

First and foremost, personal protective equipment (PPE) is non-negotiable. Safety goggles are paramount to shield eyes from flying debris, which can be propelled at high speeds when cutting, grinding, or sanding. For tasks that generate dust or particulate matter, a dust mask or respirator is crucial to prevent inhalation of potentially harmful particles. Hearing protection, such as earplugs or earmuffs, should be used during prolonged use of the tool to safeguard against noise-induced hearing loss. Additionally, wearing gloves can protect hands from abrasions and improve grip on the tool, though they should be tight-fitting to avoid catching in the tool's moving parts.

The condition and setup of the workspace itself are equally important. A well-lit and ventilated area not only ensures that fine details can be accurately worked on but also dissipates harmful dust and fumes. The work surface should be stable and clean, free of clutter that could obstruct the project or pose a fire hazard, particularly when working with flammable materials. Tools and materials should be organized and within easy reach to avoid unnecessary movements that could lead to accidents.

Another critical safety consideration is the correct use and maintenance of the Dremel tool and its accessories. Before beginning any project, inspect the tool for damage, ensuring that all parts are secure and in good working order. Attachments should be correctly fitted according to the manufacturer's instructions, and the tool should never be modified or used with incompatible accessories. Regular maintenance, including cleaning and checking for wear on attachments, extends the life of the tool and prevents malfunctions that could lead to injury.

Electrical safety is also paramount. Ensure that the workspace is dry and free from water to prevent electric shock. The use of extension cords should be minimized, and never use the tool with a damaged power cord. When not in use, the tool should be unplugged, and batteries removed from cordless models to prevent accidental activation.

Safe practices extend to the handling of materials being worked on. Secure materials with clamps or a vise to keep them from moving while being cut, drilled, or sanded. This not only prevents injury but also allows for more precise work. Be aware of the properties of the materials you are working with, especially if they are hazardous or require special handling precautions.

Lastly, educating oneself on emergency procedures is a critical aspect of workspace safety. Knowing how to quickly and efficiently respond to accidents, from minor cuts to more serious injuries, can prevent further harm. Keep a first aid kit readily available and ensure it is stocked with supplies to treat common injuries. Familiarize yourself with the quickest route to seek medical help if a serious injury occurs.

Creating and maintaining a safe workspace is fundamental when using a Dremel tool, especially for beginners. By wearing appropriate PPE, organizing and preparing the workspace, using and maintaining the tool correctly, practicing electrical safety, securing materials properly, and being prepared for emergencies, users can minimize risks and enjoy a productive and safe crafting or DIY experience.

Dremel Tool Safety Features

Dremel tools, renowned for their versatility and precision, also emphasize user safety through a range of built-in features and design considerations. These safety measures are critical for beginners to understand and appreciate, ensuring they can undertake a variety of projects without compromising on their well-being.

One of the primary safety features of a Dremel tool is its ergonomic design. The tools are crafted to fit comfortably in the user's hand, reducing fatigue and providing a firm grip to maintain control during operation. This design minimizes the risk of accidental slips or mishaps that could lead to injury.

Variable speed settings are another crucial safety aspect. Dremel tools offer a wide range of speeds, allowing users to select the most appropriate speed for the task at hand. Lower speeds are ideal for delicate tasks or materials that require precision, while higher speeds can handle tougher materials or more aggressive cutting and sanding. The ability to control speed helps prevent damage to the material being worked on and reduces the risk of the tool slipping or reacting unpredictably.

The inclusion of a collet lock is a feature that enhances safety by ensuring attachments are securely fastened before use. This lock mechanism prevents the attachment from becoming loose during operation, which could lead to accidents. Before any operation, users are advised to check that the collet lock is engaged and that the attachment is secure, a step that underscores the importance of preparation in safety protocols.

Many Dremel tools come equipped with a shield attachment designed to protect the user from flying debris and sparks. This is especially important when cutting, grinding, or sanding materials that can produce small particles that may cause injury or irritation to the eyes or skin. The shield attachment serves as a barrier, keeping these particles away from the user.

Another notable safety feature is the integrated ventilation system found in Dremel tools. This system helps to prevent the tool from overheating, a common issue with high-speed rotary tools. Overheating can not only damage the tool but also poses a burn risk to the user. The ventilation system ensures that the tool remains at a manageable temperature, even during extended use.

Dremel tools also often include a feedback control system that automatically adjusts power and speed based on the load. This feature helps to maintain performance without overloading the tool or the user, reducing the risk of unexpected jumps or movements that could lead to loss of control.

In addition to these built-in features, the importance of reading the user manual cannot be overstated. Dremel tools come with comprehensive manuals that detail all operational aspects, including safety precautions specific to the model. Familiarizing oneself with these instructions is a fundamental step in ensuring safe use.

Personal Protective Equipment (PPE) such as safety glasses, dust masks, and ear protection are recommended when using any power tool, including Dremel tools. While not built into the tool itself, the use of PPE is strongly advised in the user manuals and safety guidelines provided by Dremel, reinforcing the company's commitment to safety.

Lastly, Dremel's commitment to safety is also evident in their customer support and educational resources. They provide access to instructional materials and videos that not only guide users on how to achieve the best results with their projects but also emphasize safe practices throughout.

For beginners, understanding and utilizing these safety features is essential. By doing so, they can confidently explore the capabilities of their Dremel tool while minimizing the risk of injury, ensuring a safe and enjoyable crafting or DIY experience.

Common Safety Mistakes to Avoid

Using a Dremel tool, while exciting and versatile for a wide range of DIY projects, requires a keen understanding of safety to prevent accidents and injuries. Common safety mistakes can often be easily avoided with proper knowledge and precautions. One of the primary oversights is neglecting to wear appropriate personal protective equipment (PPE). Safety goggles are essential to protect the eyes from flying debris, dust, and particles that can result from cutting, sanding, or grinding. Similarly, neglecting ear protection can lead to hearing damage during prolonged use of high-speed rotary tools. Furthermore, wearing a dust mask or respirator is crucial when working with materials that produce fine particles or toxic fumes, ensuring that the lungs are safeguarded.

Another frequent mistake is using the tool without securing the workpiece. Unstable or unsecured materials can shift unexpectedly, leading to inaccuracies or, worse, accidents where hands or fingers are put in harm's way. Clamping down the material not only ensures precision but also enhances safety by allowing users to focus on controlling the tool without holding the workpiece by hand.

Overlooking the importance of choosing the correct attachment for the material and task at hand is also a common pitfall. Dremel tools come with a wide array of attachments and accessories designed for specific applications. Using an inappropriate attachment can not only damage the material but can also pose a risk to the user, as the tool may not operate as expected, leading to loss of control or breakage of the attachment.

Many beginners also tend to ignore the speed settings on their Dremel tool, either using too high or too low a speed for the task. High speeds can cause overheating, damage to the material, or breakage of bits and accessories, while too low speeds might result in poor performance and unnecessary physical exertion, leading to accidents. Understanding the optimal speed setting for each type of material and attachment is crucial for safe and effective use.

Failing to maintain a clean and organized workspace can lead to accidents. Debris, dust, and disorganized tools not only make it difficult to work efficiently but also increase the risk of slipping, tripping, or accidentally coming into contact with the rotary tool bit. Regularly cleaning the workspace and organizing tools and materials can significantly reduce these risks.

Underestimating the tool's power and overreaching while using it can cause users to lose balance or control, leading to potential injuries. It's important to respect the power of the Dremel tool, keeping it firmly in hand and working within a comfortable range of motion.

Lastly, neglecting regular maintenance of the Dremel tool can compromise its safety and functionality. Bits and attachments should be checked for wear and tear and replaced when necessary. The tool itself should be cleaned and inspected for any signs of damage or malfunction, ensuring it operates smoothly and safely every time it's used.

Understanding and avoiding these common safety mistakes can greatly enhance the safe use of a Dremel tool. By wearing the right PPE, securing the workpiece, selecting appropriate attachments, adjusting speed settings according to the task, maintaining an organized workspace, respecting the tool's power, and adhering to regular maintenance, beginners can enjoy a wide range of DIY projects while minimizing the risk of injury.

Getting to Know Your Dremel Tool

Parts of a Dremel Tool

A Dremel tool is comprised of several key components that work together to offer a versatile and powerful solution for a wide range of projects. Understanding these parts is crucial for beginners to maximize the tool's potential while ensuring safe and effective use.

At the heart of the Dremel tool is the motor, which powers the tool and drives its high-speed rotation. This motor is encased in the tool's body, which is designed for ease of handling and maneuverability. The body often includes a soft-grip area to enhance comfort and control during extended periods of use, reducing fatigue and improving precision.

The speed control feature is another integral part of the Dremel tool, allowing users to adjust the rotational speed of the bit or accessory. This is essential for working with different materials that require varying speeds to cut, carve, or polish effectively. For beginners, starting at lower speeds and gradually increasing is advisable as they become more accustomed to the tool's behavior and capabilities.

The chuck, also known as the collet, is where accessories and bits are attached to the tool. It's a critical component that ensures the accessory is securely held in place during operation. The Dremel tool comes with a collet nut that tightens or loosens the collet, allowing for easy changes of accessories. Some models include a keyless chuck, which facilitates even quicker and more convenient accessory changes without the need for additional tools.

Attached to the front of the Dremel tool is the nose cap, which can be removed to attach various attachments like the cutting guide or the flex shaft. The flex shaft attachment is particularly useful for detailed work, as it allows for more precise control and maneuverability in tight spaces. It essentially extends the reach of the Dremel tool, making it easier to engrave, polish, or sand in hard-to-reach areas.

The power switch, typically located on the body of the tool, is what users interact with to turn the Dremel tool on and off. Its placement is designed for easy access, allowing for quick and straightforward operation.

For corded models, the power cord is another essential part, providing the electricity needed to power the tool. Cordless models, on the other hand, include a battery compartment, usually integrated into the tool's body, making them more portable and convenient for use in areas without immediate access to power outlets.

The ventilation system is a critical safety feature, designed to prevent overheating during extended use. It consists of air vents that allow for proper airflow around the motor, ensuring the tool operates within safe temperature ranges.

Lastly, many Dremel tools come with additional accessories and attachments, each designed for specific tasks. These range from cutting wheels and drill bits to sanding bands and polishing pads. Understanding how to attach and use these components is key to leveraging the Dremel tool's full capabilities.

For beginners, familiarizing themselves with these parts and their functions is the first step toward mastering the use of the Dremel tool. With this knowledge, users can confidently tackle a variety of projects, ensuring both safety and effectiveness in their creative endeavors.

Setting Up Your Dremel for the First Time

Setting up your Dremel tool for the first time is an exciting step towards unlocking a world of DIY projects, crafting, and home improvements. The process is straightforward, designed to get you comfortable and ready to start creating with confidence. When you unbox your Dremel, you'll find the tool itself along with various attachments and accessories, depending on the model you've chosen. Your first task is to familiarize yourself with the parts and functionalities of your new tool.

Start by charging your Dremel if it's a cordless model, or simply plug it into a power source if it's corded. While it charges or before you plug it in, take this time to read through the user manual. The manual is a treasure trove of information, providing detailed instructions on assembly, use, and safety precautions. Understanding the speed settings is crucial, as different materials and projects require different speeds. Most Dremel tools have a speed range, with lower speeds suited for polishing and higher speeds ideal for cutting and carving.

Next, explore the different attachments and accessories that came with your Dremel. You might find sanding bands, cutting wheels, grinding stones, and polishing compounds, among others. Each attachment has a specific purpose and is designed to fit onto the Dremel in a unique way. Learning how to change these attachments is essential. Typically, this involves loosening the collet nut at the end of the tool, inserting the desired attachment, and then tightening the nut back in place. Some models might come with a keyless chuck, allowing for easier attachment changes.

Before you start your first project, practice attaching and removing various bits and accessories. This practice will help you become familiar with the process and ensure you know how to securely fasten each attachment. Remember, a properly attached accessory is crucial for safe and effective operation.

Understanding the pressure needed for different tasks is another important aspect of getting to know your Dremel. Applying too much pressure can damage both the tool and the material you're working on. Start with light pressure and increase gradually as needed, letting the speed of the tool do the work rather than force.

Select a simple project to start with, something that allows you to practice using different attachments and applying various speeds without the pressure of a perfect outcome. This could be something as straightforward as sanding down a piece of scrap wood or polishing an old piece of metal. The goal is to get a feel for how the Dremel behaves with different materials and tasks.

Lastly, set up a comfortable and safe workspace. Ensure you have good lighting and sufficient ventilation, especially if you'll be creating dust or fumes. Keep your Dremel and all attachments organized and within easy reach. Wearing protective gear, such as safety glasses and dust masks, is also recommended to protect yourself from potential hazards.

Setting up your Dremel tool for the first time is not just about getting it out of the box and plugging it in. It's about creating a foundation of knowledge and practice that will enable you to tackle a wide range of projects with confidence. By taking the time to understand your tool, its attachments, and how it interacts with different materials, you're setting yourself up for a rewarding journey of creativity and craftsmanship.

Maintenance and Care

Maintaining and caring for your Dremel tool is essential to ensure its longevity and optimal performance. Whether you're a beginner or have some experience under your belt, understanding how to properly maintain your Dremel will save you time and money, and keep your projects running smoothly.

The first step in Dremel maintenance is regular cleaning. After each use, it's important to remove any dust, debris, or material remnants that have accumulated on the tool and in its moving parts. A soft brush or compressed air can be used to clear the vents and crevices, preventing overheating and ensuring efficient operation. For more stubborn grime, a slightly damp cloth can wipe down the exterior, but ensure the tool is completely dry before storing it.

Checking and replacing the carbon brushes is another key aspect of Dremel care. These brushes wear down over time due to friction and will eventually need replacing. Most Dremel tools have externally accessible brushes for easy inspection and replacement. A significant decrease in power or unusual sparking from the motor area indicates it's time to check the brushes. Replacements are readily available and installing new brushes can significantly extend the life of your tool.

The collet, a small metal sleeve that holds the bit in place, requires attention as well. Over time, the collet can become clogged with debris or may wear out, affecting the tool's grip on the bits. Regularly checking the collet and collet nut for signs of wear and ensuring they are clean will improve the precision and safety of your Dremel tool. If a collet becomes damaged or excessively worn, replacing it is a simple and cost-effective way to maintain the tool's functionality.

Lubrication is crucial for parts of the Dremel that move or create friction. However, it's important to follow the manufacturer's instructions regarding lubrication. Some models are designed to operate without additional lubricants, while others may require periodic oiling. If your model does require lubrication, use only the type recommended by the manufacturer to avoid damaging the tool.

Storing your Dremel tool properly is also an important aspect of maintenance. Keep the tool in a dry, dust-free environment to prevent rust and dust accumulation. If your Dremel came with a case, use it for storage to protect the tool and keep all the accessories organized. Avoid leaving the tool in places with extreme temperature fluctuations, as this can damage the electronic components.

Finally, keeping an eye on your attachments and accessories is vital. Inspect them regularly for wear or damage, and replace any that are no longer effective. Using worn or damaged accessories can put unnecessary strain on the tool and lead to poor results or accidents.

By adhering to these maintenance and care guidelines, beginners can ensure their Dremel tool remains a reliable and effective partner in their crafting and DIY projects. Regular upkeep not only prolongs the life of the tool but also ensures it's ready and safe to use for any project, helping you to achieve the best possible outcomes with every use.

Understanding Dremel Attachments and Accessories

Overview of Dremel Attachments

Dremel tools are celebrated for their versatility, a characteristic largely attributed to the wide array of attachments and accessories available. These attachments transform the Dremel from a simple rotary tool into a multi-purpose device capable of handling a diverse range of tasks across various materials. For beginners, navigating the extensive selection of Dremel attachments and accessories can be overwhelming, yet understanding their functions is key to unlocking the tool's full potential.

The cutting accessories are among the most commonly used, equipped with specific bits designed for cutting wood, metal, plastic, and even tile. Fiberglass reinforced cut-off wheels are ideal for slicing through metal, while multipurpose cutting bits are suitable for softer materials like wood and plastic. Understanding the material compatibility of each cutting accessory ensures both safety and the longevity of the bits.

Sanding accessories come in various shapes and sizes, including sanding bands, discs, and flap wheels, each designed for different surfaces and levels of detail. Sanding bands are perfect for smoothing larger, flat surfaces or for shaping and carving. Flap wheels and sanding discs, on the other hand, allow for precision in smoothing and refining edges or for working in tight spaces.

For those interested in detailed work, engraving and carving accessories are invaluable. High-speed cutter bits and engraving cutters are crafted for precision, enabling intricate designs on wood, metal, and even glass. The choice between different shapes and sizes allows for customizability in the depth and detail of the work.

Polishing accessories, including polishing wheels, brushes, and polishing compound, bring a high shine to a variety of materials. Whether polishing metals to a mirror finish or cleaning up a vintage piece of jewelry, these accessories are essential for achieving a professional-looking result.

Grinding and sharpening accessories are designed for material removal and edge sharpening. Silicon carbide stones are excellent for sharpening, deburring, and general grinding of most materials, while aluminum oxide grinding stones are used for sharpening, smoothing, and finishing.

Drilling and routing accessories expand the Dremel's capabilities even further. Drill bits allow for precision drilling in metals, woods, and plastics, whereas routing bits are used for detailed carving, engraving, and routing in softer materials.

For cleaning and restoration projects, the Dremel offers a range of brushing and scouring accessories. Wire brushes remove rust and corrosion from metal surfaces, nylon bristle brushes are gentle on softer surfaces, and polishing brushes are used with polishing compound to bring out a high shine.

A unique category of accessories is designed for specific projects, such as the EZ Lock system, which simplifies the process of changing out cutting, sanding, and grinding accessories, making the task quick and tool-free. This system is particularly beneficial for beginners, as it reduces the complexity and time involved in switching between tasks.

Adapters and attachments, such as the flex shaft attachment, enhance the Dremel's ergonomics and accessibility. The flex shaft allows for precise control and comfort during extended use, particularly in detailed work or hard-to-reach areas. Other attachments, like the rotary tool workstation, convert the Dremel into a drill press or a tool holder for stationary work.

Understanding the vast array of Dremel attachments and accessories is crucial for beginners to fully utilize their tool. Each accessory is designed with a specific purpose in mind, enabling users to tackle a wide range of projects with precision and ease. By familiarizing themselves with these options, beginners can effectively select the right accessory for their project, ensuring successful outcomes while also expanding their skills and creative possibilities.

How to Choose the Right Attachment
for Your Project

When it comes to utilizing a Dremel tool effectively, selecting the appropriate attachment for your specific project is paramount. Understanding the diverse range of attachments available and their respective applications will not only enhance your project outcomes but also ensure safety and efficiency in your work.

Begin by familiarizing yourself with the various types of attachments that come with your Dremel tool kit. These typically include cutting wheels, sanding drums, grinding stones, engraving cutters, polishing pads, and drill bits, among others. Each attachment is designed to serve a distinct purpose and is suited for specific materials and tasks.

For precision cutting tasks, such as trimming plastic, metal, or wood, cutting wheels are indispensable. These thin, rotating discs are available in different sizes and compositions to accommodate various materials and thicknesses. Diamond-coated cutting wheels are ideal for cutting through hard materials like tile or glass, while fiberglass-reinforced cutting wheels excel in metalwork.

When it comes to shaping and smoothing surfaces, sanding drums and grinding stones are indispensable. Sanding drums, fitted with sandpaper sleeves, are perfect for smoothing rough edges, shaping contours, and removing imperfections on wood, plastic, and metal surfaces. Grinding stones, on the other hand, are designed for more aggressive material removal, such as sharpening blades or grinding down metal surfaces.

For intricate engraving and detailing work, engraving cutters are essential. These small, pointed attachments come in various shapes and sizes to accommodate different engraving styles and depths. Whether you're etching designs into metal, carving patterns into wood, or engraving text onto glass, selecting the appropriate cutter ensures precise and professional-looking results.

Polishing pads and accessories are indispensable for achieving a flawless finish on metals, plastics, and even stones. These attachments, typically made of felt or fabric, are used in conjunction with polishing compounds to restore luster and shine to surfaces, remove scratches, and achieve a mirror-like finish.

Drill bits are essential attachments for drilling precise holes in various materials, including wood, plastic, metal, and ceramics. Dremel offers a wide range of drill bit sizes and styles to accommodate different hole diameters and depths, ensuring accuracy and versatility in your drilling tasks.

When selecting the right attachment for your project, consider the material you'll be working with, the desired outcome, and the specific task at hand. Refer to the manufacturer's guidelines and recommendations for each attachment to ensure compatibility with your Dremel tool model and to maximize performance and safety.

Experimentation and practice are key to mastering the art of attachment selection with your Dremel tool. Start with small, simple projects to familiarize yourself with the capabilities of each attachment and gradually expand your skills as you gain confidence and proficiency. With the right attachment at your disposal, your Dremel tool becomes a versatile and indispensable tool for a wide range of DIY, crafting, and hobbyist projects.

Changing Attachments and Accessories

Changing attachments and accessories on your Dremel tool is a straightforward process that enhances its versatility and expands its capabilities for various projects. Whether you're transitioning from sanding to cutting or switching to a specialized accessory for engraving, understanding how to change attachments effectively is essential for beginners.

Begin by powering off and unplugging your Dremel tool for safety. Next, locate the collet nut, which is the part that secures the attachment in place. Depending on your Dremel model, the collet nut may be located at the tip of the tool or near the base where the power cord connects.

Using the provided wrench or tool, loosen the collet nut by turning it counterclockwise. Be sure not to overtighten or force the nut, as this can damage the threading or the attachment itself.

Once the collet nut is loose, gently remove the current attachment by pulling it straight out of the collet. Take care not to touch any sharp or hot surfaces, especially if the attachment was recently in use.

With the old attachment removed, select the desired accessory for your next task. Dremel offers a wide range of attachments and accessories, including cutting wheels, sanding drums, engraving bits, polishing pads, and more. Choose the appropriate accessory based on the material and type of work you plan to do.

Insert the new accessory into the collet, ensuring that it fits securely and sits flush against the collet nut. Avoid forcing the accessory into place, as this can cause damage or misalignment.

Once the accessory is in position, tighten the collet nut by turning it clockwise with the wrench or tool. Again, be careful not to overtighten, as this can damage the threading or the accessory itself. The collet nut should be snug enough to hold the accessory firmly in place without wobbling or slipping.

After securing the new attachment, double-check to ensure that it is properly aligned and seated within the collet. Inspect the attachment for any signs of damage or wear, such as bent blades or worn edges, and replace it if necessary.

Finally, plug in your Dremel tool and power it on to test the new attachment. Start with a low speed setting to familiarize yourself with the feel and performance of the accessory before proceeding with your project.

By mastering the process of changing attachments and accessories on your Dremel tool, you'll unlock its full potential and gain the confidence to tackle a wide range of tasks and projects with ease. With practice and experience, you'll become adept at swapping out accessories quickly and efficiently, making your Dremel tool a valuable companion in your creative endeavors.

Specialized Attachments for Advanced Projects

Specialized attachments are the key to unlocking the full potential of your Dremel tool, especially when undertaking advanced projects. These attachments are designed to cater to specific tasks and materials, providing precision and versatility that standard attachments may lack.

One of the most common specialized attachments is the router attachment, which allows for precise routing and shaping of wood, plastic, and even soft metals. This attachment is ideal for advanced woodworking projects, such as creating intricate designs or crafting custom cabinetry. With adjustable depth settings and a variety of router bits available, the router attachment provides the precision and control necessary for professional-quality results.

For metalworking enthusiasts, the rotary tool's flex shaft attachment is indispensable. This attachment features a flexible shaft that allows for greater maneuverability and control, making it ideal for intricate metalworking tasks such as engraving, polishing, and grinding. With the flex shaft attachment, users can access tight spaces and achieve fine details with ease, making it a must-have for advanced metalworking projects.

Another specialized attachment worth mentioning is the detailer's grip attachment, which provides additional stability and control when working on detailed projects. This attachment is particularly useful for engraving, carving, and etching, allowing users to maintain a steady hand and achieve precise results even on delicate materials. The detailer's grip attachment is a valuable tool for advanced crafters who demand precision and accuracy in their work.

For those working with ceramics or glass, the diamond wheel point attachment is essential. This attachment features a diamond-coated wheel that is capable of cutting, grinding, and etching hard materials such as glass, ceramic, and porcelain. Whether you're shaping a piece of stained glass or etching a design into a ceramic tile, the diamond wheel point attachment provides the precision and durability needed for advanced projects in these materials.

Woodworkers will also appreciate specialized attachments such as the plunge router attachment, which allows for controlled plunge cuts and grooves in wood. This attachment is ideal for advanced woodworking projects such as making mortises or creating intricate joinery. With adjustable depth settings and a sturdy base, the plunge router attachment provides the precision and stability necessary for professional-quality woodworking.

In addition to these specialized attachments, there are also a variety of accessories available that can enhance the functionality of your Dremel tool for advanced projects. These accessories include specialty sanding drums, polishing pads, cutting wheels, and grinding stones, each designed to tackle specific tasks with precision and efficiency.

Overall, specialized attachments play a crucial role in expanding the capabilities of your Dremel tool for advanced projects. Whether you're working with wood, metal, ceramics, or glass, there's a specialized attachment available to help you achieve professional-quality results with precision and ease. By investing in these attachments and accessories, you can take your crafting to the next level and tackle even the most challenging projects with confidence and skill.

Basic Techniques and Skills

Sanding and Smoothing

Sanding and smoothing are fundamental techniques that beginners should master when using a Dremel tool. These techniques are essential for preparing surfaces, refining shapes, and achieving a polished finish on various materials such as wood, metal, plastic, and more.

To begin, select the appropriate sanding attachment for your Dremel tool. Sanding drums, sanding bands, and abrasive buffs are commonly used attachments for sanding and smoothing tasks. The grit of the sanding attachment determines its aggressiveness, with lower grit numbers being more coarse and higher grit numbers providing a finer finish.

Before starting, ensure that the workpiece is securely clamped down to prevent movement during sanding. Safety goggles and a dust mask should also be worn to protect against flying debris and dust particles.

Start the Dremel tool at a low speed to familiarize yourself with the handling and control. Slowly guide the sanding attachment across the surface of the material, applying gentle and even pressure. Keep the tool moving to prevent uneven sanding and avoid overheating the material.

For flat surfaces, use a back-and-forth motion, overlapping each pass slightly to ensure even coverage. For curved or irregular shapes, move the tool in a circular motion to conform to the contours of the material.

As you sand, periodically check the surface for smoothness and consistency. Pay attention to any rough patches or imperfections that may require additional sanding.

To achieve a smooth finish, gradually increase the speed of the Dremel tool and switch to a finer grit sanding attachment. This allows for finer control and precision in smoothing out any remaining roughness or scratches.

For intricate or hard-to-reach areas, consider using smaller sanding accessories such as sanding bands or abrasive buffs. These attachments provide greater maneuverability and precision for detailing work.

Once sanding is complete, inspect the surface for any remaining imperfections. Minor scratches or blemishes can be further refined using finer grit sanding attachments or polishing accessories.

After sanding, it's important to clean the workpiece thoroughly to remove any dust or debris. This ensures a clean surface for finishing or painting.

Sanding and smoothing are essential techniques for beginners using a Dremel tool. By selecting the appropriate attachments, mastering control and speed, and paying attention to detail, you can achieve professional-quality results on a variety of materials. With practice and patience, sanding and smoothing with a Dremel tool can open up a world of possibilities for your crafting and DIY projects.

Cutting and Carving

Cutting and carving are fundamental techniques when using a Dremel tool, offering beginners a gateway to unlocking the tool's versatility and precision. Whether working with wood, metal, plastic, or other materials, mastering these techniques allows users to create intricate designs, precise shapes, and custom details with ease.

When cutting with a Dremel tool, it's essential to choose the right cutting bit for the material and project at hand. For example, a high-speed cutter bit is suitable for cutting through wood, while a reinforced cutting wheel is better suited for metals. Before starting, ensure the workpiece is securely clamped or held in place to prevent movement and ensure safety.

To begin cutting, set the Dremel tool to the appropriate speed based on the material being cut and the type of cutting bit being used. Start with a lower speed for more control, then gradually increase as needed for faster cutting. Hold the Dremel tool firmly with both hands, positioning the cutting bit at a slight angle to the surface of the material. Apply gentle pressure and let the tool do the work, allowing the cutting bit to make smooth, steady progress through the material.

When carving with a Dremel tool, precision and control are key. Start by selecting the appropriate carving bit based on the desired depth and detail of the carving. For intricate designs, a smaller, finer carving bit may be preferable, while larger bits are suitable for removing material more quickly.

Before carving, sketch the design onto the material using a pencil or marker to serve as a guide. Secure the workpiece in place to prevent movement during carving, then set the Dremel tool to the desired speed based on the material and carving bit being used. Begin carving slowly, following the outline of the design and gradually increasing pressure as needed to achieve the desired depth.

As you carve, periodically stop to remove excess material and dust buildup, ensuring a clean and precise finish. Take your time and work carefully, adjusting speed and pressure as needed to maintain control and accuracy. For detailed areas or tight curves, consider using a smaller carving bit or switching to a different type of bit for better maneuverability.

Once the carving is complete, use sanding attachments or abrasive bits to smooth rough edges and refine the details of the carving. Take care to remove any remaining dust or debris from the workpiece before proceeding with finishing or painting.

Cutting and carving with a Dremel tool offer beginners the opportunity to create intricate designs and precise shapes across a variety of materials. By selecting the right cutting and carving bits, mastering speed and pressure control, and working carefully and methodically, beginners can achieve professional-quality results and unlock the full potential of their Dremel tool.

Engraving and Etching

Engraving and etching with a Dremel tool are versatile techniques that allow beginners to add personalized touches to various materials, including metal, glass, wood, and plastic. These techniques are relatively simple to learn but can yield impressive results when executed with precision and care.

To begin engraving or etching with a Dremel tool, it's essential to select the appropriate engraving bit or accessory based on the material you plan to work with. For example, carbide or diamond-tipped bits are suitable for harder materials like metal and glass, while high-speed steel bits are better suited for softer materials like wood and plastic.

Before starting, ensure that your workpiece is securely clamped or held in place to prevent movement during the engraving process. Additionally, consider practicing on a scrap piece of material to familiarize yourself with the pressure and speed required for optimal results.

When engraving or etching, maintain a steady hand and apply consistent pressure to achieve uniform depth and clarity in your designs. Start with light passes, gradually increasing pressure as needed to achieve the desired depth of engraving. Keep in mind that it's easier to remove material than to add it back, so err on the side of caution when engraving intricate designs.

Experiment with different speeds and techniques to achieve varying effects in your engravings. Higher speeds are typically used for fine lines and delicate details, while lower speeds are suitable for broader strokes and shading effects. Additionally, adjusting the depth of the engraving bit can create varying levels of texture and dimension in your designs.

When etching on glass or metal surfaces, consider using a stencil or template to guide your designs and ensure accuracy. Apply a small amount of lubricant, such as water or cutting oil, to the surface to prevent overheating and minimize friction during the etching process.

After completing your engraving or etching, carefully clean the workpiece to remove any debris or residue left behind. Depending on the material, you may need to use a gentle solvent or abrasive cleaner to achieve a polished finish.

Finally, practice patience and persistence when mastering engraving and etching techniques with a Dremel tool. Like any skill, proficiency develops over time with practice and experience. Take your time to experiment with different materials, designs, and techniques to discover the full potential of your Dremel tool for engraving and etching projects. With dedication and creativity, you'll soon be adding personalized touches to your creations with confidence and precision.

Polishing and Cleaning

Polishing and cleaning are essential techniques that beginners can easily master with a Dremel tool, adding a professional finish to their projects and restoring the shine to various surfaces. Polishing involves smoothing and refining a surface to achieve a glossy or reflective finish, while cleaning entails removing dirt, grime, and oxidation buildup to restore the appearance of materials. With the right attachments and techniques, beginners can effectively polish and clean a wide range of materials, including metals, plastics, ceramics, and even glass.

When it comes to polishing with a Dremel tool, selecting the appropriate attachment is crucial. Felt polishing wheels are commonly used for applying polishing compounds and achieving a high shine on metals and plastics. Beginners should start by attaching a felt wheel to their Dremel tool and applying a small amount of polishing compound to the surface. Working at a low speed, gently move the Dremel tool across the surface in circular motions, gradually increasing speed and pressure as desired results are achieved. It's important to keep the tool moving to prevent overheating and ensure an even finish.

For larger surfaces or intricate details, cone-shaped polishing tips can be used to access tight spaces and contours. These tips are particularly effective for polishing jewelry, small metal components, and decorative objects. Similarly, abrasive polishing discs can be attached to the

Dremel tool for more aggressive polishing tasks, such as removing scratches or blemishes from metal surfaces. Beginners should exercise caution when using abrasive discs to avoid removing too much material and causing damage to the surface.

In addition to polishing, the Dremel tool is also a versatile tool for cleaning various surfaces. Wire brush attachments are commonly used for removing rust, paint, and corrosion from metal surfaces. Beginners should select the appropriate wire brush attachment based on the material and level of cleaning required, ensuring that the bristles are not too stiff to avoid scratching the surface. When using wire brushes, it's important to work at a low speed and apply gentle pressure to prevent damage to the surface.

For cleaning delicate materials such as jewelry, glass, and ceramics, soft-bristle brushes or polishing wheels can be used to gently remove dirt and grime without causing damage. Beginners should use a mild cleaning solution or water with a small amount of dish soap to lubricate the surface and aid in the cleaning process. When cleaning intricate details or hard-to-reach areas, small polishing tips or brushes can be attached to the Dremel tool to ensure thorough cleaning without damaging delicate surfaces.

Overall, polishing and cleaning with a Dremel tool offer beginners the opportunity to achieve professional results with ease. By selecting the appropriate attachments and techniques, beginners can effectively polish and clean a wide range of materials, from metals and plastics to glass and ceramics. With practice and attention to detail, beginners can enhance the appearance of their projects and restore the beauty of various surfaces using their Dremel tool.

Drilling and Hollowing

Drilling and hollowing are fundamental techniques that beginners can quickly master with a Dremel tool, expanding their repertoire of DIY skills. The Dremel's precision and versatility make it an ideal tool for drilling small holes and hollowing out various materials, from wood to plastic to soft metals.

To begin, select the appropriate drill bit for your project. Dremel offers a variety of drill bit options, including high-speed cutters, diamond-coated bits for hard materials, and carbide bits for soft materials. Choose a bit size that matches the diameter of the hole you need to drill.

Before starting, ensure that the material you are drilling into is securely clamped or held in place. This prevents it from moving or slipping during the drilling process, ensuring accuracy and safety.

Next, set the Dremel tool to the appropriate speed for the material and bit being used. Higher speeds are generally used for softer materials, while lower speeds are preferred for harder materials to prevent overheating and damage.

With the Dremel tool powered on, gently press the drill bit against the surface of the material at a 90-degree angle. Apply steady, even pressure as you begin drilling, allowing the bit to gradually penetrate the material. Avoid forcing the bit or applying excessive pressure, as this can lead to overheating and damage to both the bit and the material.

As you drill, periodically withdraw the bit to clear away any debris or shavings that may accumulate in the hole. This helps maintain a clean and precise drilling operation.

Once the hole has been drilled to the desired depth, carefully withdraw the bit from the material, taking care not to damage the edges of the hole. If necessary, use a small file or sandpaper attachment on the Dremel tool to smooth any rough edges around the hole.

Hollowing out materials with a Dremel tool follows a similar process but involves removing material from within an existing cavity rather than drilling a hole. This technique is commonly used in woodworking to create recesses or channels for wiring, as well as in crafting to carve out intricate designs or shapes.

To hollow out a material, select a suitable hollowing bit or attachment for the Dremel tool. These may include rotary rasp bits, carbide burrs, or specialized hollowing attachments designed for specific applications.

Once again, ensure that the material is securely clamped or held in place before beginning. With the Dremel tool set to the appropriate speed, gently guide the hollowing bit into the material, gradually removing material from within the cavity.

Use light, controlled movements to hollow out the material, periodically checking the depth and shape of the cavity to ensure accuracy. Take care not to remove too much material at once, as this can lead to uneven or unintended results.

As with drilling, periodically clear away any debris or shavings that accumulate within the cavity to maintain a clean and precise hollowing operation.

Once the desired depth and shape have been achieved, carefully withdraw the hollowing bit from the material, taking care not to damage the edges or walls of the cavity. Use a small file or sandpaper attachment on the Dremel tool to smooth any rough surfaces or refine the shape of the hollowed-out area.

By mastering the techniques of drilling and hollowing with a Dremel tool, beginners can unlock a world of creative possibilities, from simple home improvement projects to intricate woodworking and crafting endeavors. With practice and patience, these fundamental skills will become valuable tools in any DIY enthusiast's arsenal, empowering them to tackle a wide range of projects with confidence and precision.

Setting Up Your Workspace

Choosing the Right Workspace

When setting up your workspace for using a Dremel tool, it's crucial to create a safe, organized, and efficient environment that enhances your productivity and minimizes the risk of accidents. Here are some considerations to keep in mind when choosing the right workspace:

1. **Location**: Select a well-ventilated area with good lighting to ensure visibility and comfort during your work sessions. Ideally, choose a space away from distractions and where you can focus entirely on your projects without interruptions.

2. **Surface**: Opt for a sturdy and level work surface that can withstand the vibrations and movements associated with using a Dremel tool. A workbench or table made of wood or metal is preferable, as it provides stability and prevents the tool from slipping or tipping over.

3. **Protection**: Cover your work surface with a protective layer, such as a rubber mat or cardboard, to prevent damage from flying debris or accidental spills. This layer also helps absorb vibrations, reducing noise and ensuring a more comfortable working experience.

4. **Organization**: Keep your workspace clutter-free by organizing your tools, accessories, and materials in designated storage containers or drawers. This not only improves efficiency by keeping everything within reach but also reduces the risk of accidents caused by tripping over scattered items.

5. **Accessibility**: Arrange your workspace in a way that allows easy access to power outlets for plugging in your Dremel tool and other electronic devices. Consider using extension cords or power strips to ensure sufficient reach without creating hazards from tangled cables.

6. **Ventilation**: Ensure adequate ventilation in your workspace to dissipate dust, fumes, and odors generated during sanding, cutting, or polishing tasks. If working indoors, open windows or use a portable fan to promote air circulation and maintain a comfortable working environment.

7. **Personal Protective Equipment (PPE)**: Always wear appropriate PPE, such as safety glasses, a dust mask, and hearing protection, to protect yourself from potential hazards associated with using a Dremel tool. Additionally, avoid loose-fitting clothing or jewelry that could get caught in the tool's moving parts.

8. **Lighting**: Install adequate lighting above your workspace to illuminate your projects and ensure optimal visibility, especially when

working on detailed or intricate tasks. Consider using adjustable task lighting or LED lamps to direct light precisely where it's needed.

9. **Distractions**: Minimize distractions in your workspace by turning off or silencing electronic devices, such as phones or TVs, that may divert your attention away from your projects. Create a dedicated space for focused work, free from unnecessary noise or disruptions.

10. **Cleanliness**: Regularly clean and maintain your workspace to remove dust, debris, and spills that can accumulate over time. A clean and organized workspace not only promotes safety and efficiency but also fosters a sense of pride and satisfaction in your work environment.

By carefully considering these factors and tailoring your workspace to suit your specific needs and preferences, you can create an ideal environment for using a Dremel tool effectively and safely. Whether you're embarking on a new DIY project or honing your skills as a craftsman, a well-designed workspace sets the stage for success and creativity.

Organizing Your Tools and Accessories

Organizing your tools and accessories is a crucial aspect of setting up your workspace for Dremel projects, especially for beginners. A well-organized workspace not only enhances efficiency but also ensures safety and ease of access to necessary tools and materials.

Begin by designating a dedicated workspace for your Dremel projects. Ideally, choose a well-lit area with sufficient ventilation to ensure comfort and safety during extended periods of use. A sturdy workbench or table provides a stable surface for working with your Dremel tool.

Invest in storage solutions such as toolboxes, shelves, or organizers to keep your Dremel tool and accessories neatly arranged and easily accessible. Consider organizing your tools and accessories based on their frequency of use or type of project. For example, keep commonly used attachments within arm's reach, while less frequently used ones can be stored in labeled containers or drawers.

Utilize small containers or trays to store small accessories such as collets, mandrels, and cutting wheels. Clear, labeled containers make it easy to identify and retrieve the necessary accessories for each project, minimizing time spent searching for tools and reducing frustration.

For larger accessories such as sanding drums or cutting guides, consider utilizing wall-mounted storage solutions or pegboards. This not only saves valuable workspace but also keeps these items within sight and easily accessible.

To prevent clutter and maintain a safe working environment, regularly clean and organize your workspace. Dispose of any debris or unused materials, and return tools and accessories to their designated storage locations after each use.

Consider investing in additional organizational tools such as magnetic strips or tool racks to maximize space efficiency and keep your workspace tidy. These tools can be particularly useful for organizing small metal accessories or frequently used tools such as wrenches and screwdrivers.

Lastly, don't forget to incorporate safety measures into your workspace organization. Keep flammable materials away from heat sources, ensure electrical cords are properly secured and away from sharp edges, and always follow manufacturer guidelines for storing and handling your Dremel tool and accessories.

Creating a Safe and Efficient Work Environment

When it comes to using a Dremel tool, creating a safe and efficient work environment is paramount, especially for beginners. Setting up your workspace properly ensures not only your safety but also enhances productivity and the quality of your work.

Begin by selecting an appropriate workspace. Choose a well-lit area with adequate ventilation to minimize dust and fumes. A dedicated workbench or sturdy table is ideal, providing a stable surface for your projects. Ensure the workspace is clutter-free, with tools and materials organized and within easy reach. This not only improves efficiency but also reduces the risk of accidents caused by tripping over objects.

Before starting any project, familiarize yourself with the Dremel tool's safety features and ensure they are in proper working condition. Always wear appropriate personal protective equipment (PPE), including safety glasses or goggles to protect your eyes from debris, and a dust mask to prevent inhalation of dust particles.

Secure your workpiece firmly in place using clamps or a vice to prevent it from moving during operation. This ensures precision and reduces the risk of accidents caused by the workpiece slipping or shifting unexpectedly.

When working with materials that produce dust or debris, such as wood or metal, consider using a dust collection system or setting up a makeshift barrier to contain the particles. This helps maintain a clean and safe workspace, reducing the risk of respiratory issues and minimizing cleanup time.

Position yourself ergonomically to maintain comfort and reduce fatigue during prolonged periods of use. Ensure the Dremel tool's power cord is positioned away from the work area to prevent accidental tangling or tripping.

Keep a fire extinguisher nearby in case of emergencies, especially when working with flammable materials or near electrical outlets. Familiarize yourself with its operation and ensure it is easily accessible in the event of a fire.

Regularly inspect your Dremel tool and accessories for signs of wear or damage, such as frayed cords or dull cutting bits. Replace worn parts promptly to maintain optimal performance and safety.

Lastly, always adhere to the manufacturer's instructions and recommended guidelines for safe operation of the Dremel tool. Take breaks as needed to prevent fatigue and maintain focus on your work.

By following these guidelines and setting up a safe and efficient work environment, beginners can confidently explore the endless possibilities of the Dremel tool while minimizing risks and maximizing their creative potential.

Step-by-Step Beginner Projects

Project 1: Personalizing Wooden Kitchen Utensils

For our first beginner project, we will delve into the art of personalizing wooden kitchen utensils using a Dremel tool. This project is perfect for those new to using a Dremel, as it allows for creativity while honing basic skills in engraving and detailing. Here's a step-by-step guide to personalize your wooden kitchen utensils:

Step 1: Gather Your Materials

- Wooden kitchen utensils (spoons, spatulas, etc.)
- Dremel rotary tool
- Engraving or carving attachment (such as a high-speed cutter)
- Masking tape
- Pencil
- Sandpaper (optional)

Step 2: Prepare Your Workspace

- Find a well-lit and ventilated workspace.
- Lay down a protective covering to catch any wood shavings or dust.
- Ensure your Dremel tool is fully charged and attachments are securely fitted.

Step 3: Design Your Personalization

- Use a pencil to lightly sketch your desired design onto the wooden utensil.
- Keep the design simple if you're a beginner, such as initials, simple shapes, or basic patterns.
- If you're unsure, practice your design on a spare piece of wood first.

Step 4: Secure the Utensil

- Use masking tape to secure the wooden utensil to your work surface.
- This prevents it from moving while you're engraving and helps protect the surface from scratches.

Step 5: Begin Engraving

- Attach the engraving or carving bit to your Dremel tool.

- Start engraving your design onto the wooden utensil, following the pencil marks as a guide.

- Use a steady hand and apply gentle pressure to control the depth and precision of your engraving.

- Take breaks if needed to avoid hand fatigue.

Step 6: Add Detailing (Optional)

- Once the main design is engraved, you can add additional detailing to enhance the personalization.

- Experiment with different engraving depths and patterns to create texture and interest.

- Be creative and let your imagination guide you, but remember to keep it simple if you're a beginner.

Step 7: Clean Up and Finish

- Once you're satisfied with your engraving, remove any remaining pencil marks with an eraser.

- Use sandpaper to smooth any rough edges or uneven surfaces if desired.

- Wipe down the wooden utensil with a clean cloth to remove any dust or debris.

- Optionally, you can apply a food-safe finish such as mineral oil to protect the wood and enhance its appearance.

Step 8: Admire Your Handiwork

- Once the finish is dry, step back and admire your personalized wooden kitchen utensil.
- Your unique design adds a personal touch to your cooking experience and makes a great conversation piece when entertaining guests.
- Repeat the process with other wooden utensils to create a matching set or to give as thoughtful handmade gifts.

This project not only introduces you to the basic techniques of using a Dremel tool but also allows you to unleash your creativity and personalize everyday items in your home. With practice, you'll gain confidence and skills that will inspire you to tackle more challenging projects in the future.

Project 2: Creating Custom Pet Tags

For the second beginner project, let's dive into creating custom pet tags using the versatile Dremel tool. This project not only allows beginners to practice engraving and etching but also results in personalized and functional items for beloved furry friends.

Step 1: Gather Materials

Gather the necessary materials for this project:

- Blank metal pet tags
- Dremel rotary tool
- Engraving or etching attachment (such as a carbide engraving bit)
- Safety goggles
- Marker or pencil
- Protective gloves

Step 2: Design Your Pet Tag

Using a marker or pencil, sketch out your design on the blank metal pet tag. Consider your pet's name, any decorative elements, and contact information (such as your phone number) that you want to include on the tag.

Step 3: Prepare Your Workspace

Set up a clean and well-lit workspace. Place the metal pet tag on a stable surface, ensuring it won't move around while you work. Put on your safety goggles and protective gloves to protect your eyes and hands during the engraving process.

Step 4: Attach Engraving Bit to Dremel Tool

Select an appropriate engraving or etching attachment for your Dremel tool. Attach it securely according to the manufacturer's instructions. Ensure the Dremel tool is switched off and unplugged before attaching or removing any accessories.

Step 5: Begin Engraving

With the Dremel tool set to a low speed, begin engraving your design onto the metal pet tag. Use gentle, controlled movements to trace over the lines of your sketch, gradually etching them into the metal surface. Take your time and work slowly to ensure accuracy and precision.

Step 6: Add Details

Once the main outlines of your design are engraved, you can add finer details and embellishments as desired. Experiment with different pressure levels and angles to create depth and texture in your design. The Dremel tool's versatility allows for intricate detailing and customization.

Step 7: Double-Check Information

Before finishing the engraving process, double-check the accuracy of any contact information or text you've included on the pet tag. Ensure all details are spelled correctly and clearly visible.

Step 8: Clean Up

Once you're satisfied with your engraving, switch off the Dremel tool and remove the engraving attachment. Carefully wipe away any metal shavings or debris from the pet tag using a soft cloth. Inspect the tag for any rough edges or imperfections and smooth them out if necessary.

Step 9: Attach to Pet's Collar

Finally, attach the custom pet tag to your furry friend's collar using the appropriate fastening method. Ensure it's securely attached and won't easily come loose during your pet's adventures.

Step 10: Admire Your Handiwork

Step back and admire your custom pet tag creation! Not only have you learned valuable engraving skills with your Dremel tool, but you've also crafted a personalized accessory that your pet can proudly wear wherever they go.

This project serves as a perfect introduction to the capabilities of the Dremel tool for beginners, combining practicality with creativity to produce a functional and meaningful item. With this newfound skill, you can continue to explore the possibilities of engraving and etching across various materials, expanding your repertoire of DIY projects.

Project 3: Upcycling a Vintage Frame

This project combines creativity with practicality, breathing new life into an old piece while honing your skills with the Dremel tool. Follow these step-by-step instructions to transform a vintage frame into a unique work of art:

Step 1: Gather Your Materials

- Vintage frame
- Sanding attachment for Dremel tool
- Polishing attachment for Dremel tool
- Engraving attachment for Dremel tool
- Protective eyewear
- Work gloves
- Dust mask
- Soft cloth

Step 2: Prepare Your Workspace

- Choose a well-ventilated area with a sturdy work surface.
- Lay down newspaper or a drop cloth to protect surfaces from dust and debris.
- Put on your protective eyewear, work gloves, and dust mask to ensure safety.

Step 3: Sanding

- Attach the sanding attachment to your Dremel tool.
- Carefully sand the surface of the vintage frame to remove any existing finish or imperfections.
- Start with a low speed setting on the Dremel tool and gradually increase speed as needed.
- Use gentle, circular motions to achieve an even finish.

Step 4: Polishing

- Switch to the polishing attachment on your Dremel tool.
- Apply a small amount of polishing compound to the surface of the frame.
- Using a medium speed setting, buff the frame in circular motions until it shines.
- Wipe away any excess compound with a soft cloth.

Step 5: Design and Engraving

- Plan out your design for the frame. This could include intricate patterns, initials, or decorative elements.
- Attach the engraving attachment to your Dremel tool.
- Carefully engrave your design onto the surface of the frame, using a steady hand and controlled movements.
- Experiment with different speeds and depths to achieve the desired effect.

Step 6: Final Touches

- Once you're satisfied with your engraving, wipe away any excess dust or debris from the frame.

- Inspect the frame for any areas that may need additional sanding or polishing.

- Use a soft cloth to apply a final coat of polish, buffing the frame to a beautiful shine.

Step 7: Display Your Masterpiece

- Find the perfect spot to showcase your upcycled vintage frame.

- Insert a favorite photograph or artwork into the frame to complete the transformation.

- Stand back and admire your handiwork, knowing that you've turned a forgotten piece into a stunning focal point.

With this project, you've not only learned how to use a Dremel tool for sanding, polishing, and engraving, but you've also discovered the joy of upcycling and breathing new life into old treasures. So go ahead, unleash your creativity, and let your imagination soar as you continue your journey with your Dremel tool.

Project 4: Making a Simple Jewelry Piece

This project allows newcomers to familiarize themselves with the basic techniques of shaping, engraving, and polishing while producing a beautiful accessory that can be worn or gifted.

Materials Needed:

1. Small piece of metal (such as copper or brass)
2. Jewelry findings (e.g., jump rings, clasps)
3. Chain or cord for necklace/bracelet
4. Dremel tool
5. Sanding drum attachment
6. Engraving or carving attachment
7. Polishing attachment or compound
8. Safety goggles
9. Work gloves
10. Workbench or stable surface

Step-by-Step Guide:

1. Design Your Jewelry Piece: Begin by sketching out your design on the metal piece using a pencil. Keep the design simple for your first project, such as a basic shape or a word/initials.

2. Secure the Metal: Place the metal piece securely on your workbench or stable surface using clamps or a vice to prevent it from moving while you work.

3. Sanding: Attach a sanding drum to your Dremel tool and begin sanding the surface of the metal piece. This will smooth out any rough edges and create a clean surface for engraving.

4. Engraving/Carving: Switch to an engraving or carving attachment on your Dremel tool. Carefully follow the design you sketched earlier, engraving it onto the metal surface. Start with light pressure and gradually increase as needed, ensuring precision and control over your lines.

5. Polishing: Once you've finished engraving your design, switch to a polishing attachment or apply polishing compound directly to a polishing attachment. Polish the entire surface of the metal piece, including the engraved areas, until it achieves a smooth and shiny finish.

6. Adding Findings: Once your jewelry piece is polished to your satisfaction, attach jewelry findings such as jump rings and clasps to turn it into a wearable accessory. Use pliers to open and close the jump rings securely.

7. Attach Chain/Cord: Finally, attach a chain or cord to your jewelry piece using the jump rings. Choose a chain or cord that complements the design of your jewelry piece and adjust the length as desired.

8. Final Touches: Inspect your jewelry piece for any imperfections or rough edges. Use fine-grit sandpaper or a polishing cloth to smooth out any remaining rough spots.

9. Safety Precautions: Throughout the project, remember to wear safety goggles to protect your eyes from debris, and work gloves to protect your hands from the heat generated by the Dremel tool.

10. Enjoy Your Creation: Once completed, admire your handcrafted jewelry piece and wear it with pride or gift it to a loved one. This project not only serves as an introduction to using a Dremel tool but also allows you to create a personalized piece of jewelry that reflects your creativity and craftsmanship.

Project 5: Building and Decorating a Birdhouse

This project not only allows beginners to apply their newfound skills with the Dremel tool but also results in a charming addition to any garden or outdoor space.

Step 1: Gathering Materials

Before diving into the project, gather the necessary materials:

- Pre-cut wooden birdhouse kit (readily available at craft stores)
- Dremel tool
- Sanding attachment
- Cutting attachment
- Engraving attachment
- Paints and brushes
- Wood glue
- Optional: Decorative embellishments like beads, buttons, or mosaic tiles

Step 2: Assembly

Follow the instructions provided with the birdhouse kit to assemble the basic structure. Use wood glue to secure the pieces together, ensuring a sturdy construction. Allow the glue to dry completely before proceeding to the next step.

Step 3: Sanding

Attach a sanding attachment to your Dremel tool and smooth out any rough edges or uneven surfaces on the birdhouse. Sand both the exterior and interior surfaces until they are smooth to the touch. Take care to remove any splinters or sharp points that could harm the birds.

Step 4: Cutting Entry Hole

Using a cutting attachment on your Dremel tool, carefully cut a small entry hole near the top of one side of the birdhouse. The size of the entry hole will depend on the type of birds you wish to attract. Refer to a birdhouse guide for recommended sizes.

Step 5: Decorating

This is where your creativity can truly shine. Use the engraving attachment on your Dremel tool to add decorative designs, patterns, or even the name of the lucky feathered tenants to the exterior of the birdhouse. Take your time and enjoy the process of personalizing your creation.

Step 6: Painting

Once you're satisfied with the engraving, it's time to add color. Use paints and brushes to decorate the exterior of the birdhouse. Consider using weather-resistant paint to ensure durability outdoors. Let your imagination run wild as you add vibrant colors and intricate details to your masterpiece.

Step 7: Adding Embellishments (Optional)

For an extra touch of whimsy, consider adding decorative embellishments to your birdhouse. Glue on beads, buttons, or mosaic tiles to create a unique and eye-catching design. Just be sure to use outdoor-safe adhesive to ensure that your embellishments stay in place.

Step 8: Final Touches

Once the paint and glue have dried completely, give your birdhouse a final inspection. Make any necessary touch-ups or adjustments to ensure that it's perfect for its feathered inhabitants. Then, find the perfect spot in your garden or backyard to hang your birdhouse and await the arrival of its new occupants.

With Project 5 complete, you've not only honed your skills with the Dremel tool but also created a beautiful and functional piece of art for your outdoor space. Whether you're a novice crafter or a seasoned DIY enthusiast, building and decorating a birdhouse is a rewarding and enjoyable project that's sure to bring joy to both you and the birds that call it home.

Troubleshooting Common Issues

Overcoming Technical Difficulties with the Tool

Encountering technical difficulties with your Dremel tool can be frustrating, especially for beginners eager to dive into their projects. However, understanding common issues and knowing how to troubleshoot them can save time, effort, and frustration.

One common issue beginners may face is the Dremel tool not turning on. Before panicking, ensure the tool is properly plugged in and that the power source is functioning. Check the power cord for any damage or loose connections. If the tool still doesn't turn on, it may be a problem with the switch or internal wiring, in which case contacting customer support or seeking professional repair may be necessary.

Another issue is the Dremel tool overheating during use. This often occurs when the tool is used continuously for an extended period or when it is overloaded with a heavy workload. To prevent overheating, take regular breaks during use and avoid pushing the tool beyond its limits. Additionally, ensure proper ventilation around the tool to dissipate heat effectively.

Uneven or erratic performance can also be a common issue, particularly with older or heavily used Dremel tools. This may manifest as inconsistent speed, vibration, or unusual noises during operation. In such cases, it's essential to check the tool's accessories, particularly the attachment or bit, for signs of wear or damage. Cleaning and lubricating the tool's moving parts can also help improve performance.

If the Dremel tool produces excessive vibration or noise, it may indicate a problem with the motor or bearings. Inspect the tool for any loose or damaged components, such as screws or housing, and tighten or replace them as necessary. If the issue persists, it may require professional servicing to diagnose and repair internal components.

Poor cutting or engraving performance can be frustrating, especially when working on delicate or detailed projects. Ensure the tool's speed and pressure settings are appropriate for the material and task at hand. Using a dull or worn-out cutting or engraving bit can also affect performance, so regularly inspect and replace accessories as needed.

Finally, intermittent power or electrical issues can disrupt workflow and compromise project quality. Check the power cord, plug, and outlet for any signs of damage or wear. Ensure the power source provides a stable voltage and current to prevent fluctuations that can damage the tool's electronics.

By familiarizing yourself with these common technical difficulties and their solutions, you can confidently troubleshoot issues that may arise while using your Dremel tool. Remember to prioritize safety at all times and seek professional assistance if you encounter complex or persistent problems beyond your expertise. With patience and practice, you'll overcome any technical challenges and unleash the full potential of your Dremel tool in your creative endeavors.

Fixing Mistakes on Your Projects

When working on projects with a Dremel tool, it's not uncommon to encounter mistakes or unexpected issues along the way. However, knowing how to address these mishaps can save both time and frustration. Here are some common mistakes beginners may encounter when using a Dremel tool and how to fix them:

1. **Uneven or Rough Surfaces**: If you find that the surface you're working on is uneven or rough after using the Dremel tool, it may be due to inconsistent pressure or speed. To fix this, ensure that you maintain a steady hand and apply consistent pressure as you work. Additionally, adjusting the speed of the Dremel tool to a lower setting can help achieve smoother results, especially when working with delicate materials.

2. **Accidental Overcutting or Engraving**: If you accidentally cut too deep or engrave beyond the intended area, don't panic. You can try using sanding attachments or abrasive pads to gently remove excess material and blend the mistake into the surrounding surface. Take your time and work gradually to avoid making the mistake worse.

3. **Broken Attachments or Accessories**: If an attachment or accessory breaks while in use, stop immediately to prevent further damage. Inspect the broken part to determine if it can be repaired or

if it needs to be replaced. Most Dremel attachments are designed to be easily replaced, so consult the user manual or contact customer support for guidance on obtaining a replacement.

4. Overheating or Burning: Overheating or burning of the material being worked on can occur if the Dremel tool is used at too high a speed or with too much pressure. If you notice signs of burning, such as smoke or discoloration, immediately stop using the tool and allow it to cool down. Once cooled, assess the damage and determine if the project can be salvaged by sanding away the burnt area or starting over with a fresh piece of material.

5. Inaccurate Drilling or Cutting: If your drilling or cutting isn't as precise as desired, double-check the alignment of the Dremel tool and the material being worked on. Ensure that the tool is held at the correct angle and that the accessory is properly secured. If necessary, use a guide or template to help maintain accuracy. Additionally, practicing on scrap material before starting the actual project can help improve your technique and reduce mistakes.

6. Difficulty Controlling the Tool: If you find it challenging to control the Dremel tool, especially when working on intricate details or curves, try using a lighter grip and practicing with different hand positions to find what works best for you. Additionally, using a lower speed setting can help improve control, especially for beginners who may be more comfortable with slower speeds until they gain confidence and experience.

7. **Excessive Vibration or Noise**: Excessive vibration or noise coming from the Dremel tool can indicate a problem with the tool itself or the attachment being used. Check to ensure that all components are securely tightened and properly aligned. If the issue persists, it may be necessary to clean or lubricate the tool's moving parts or seek professional assistance for further troubleshooting.

By being aware of these common mistakes and knowing how to address them, beginners can confidently tackle projects with their Dremel tool, knowing that they have the skills and knowledge to overcome any challenges that may arise. Remember, practice makes perfect, so don't be discouraged by mistakes—use them as opportunities to learn and improve your skills.

Maintenance Troubleshooting

Maintenance troubleshooting is a crucial aspect of using a Dremel tool for beginners, as proper care ensures the tool remains in optimal condition for years to come. While Dremel tools are known for their durability and reliability, occasional issues may arise that require troubleshooting and maintenance. By understanding common problems and their solutions, beginners can keep their Dremel tools in top shape and avoid unnecessary downtime.

One common issue beginners may encounter is the Dremel tool not turning on or losing power intermittently. This could be due to a variety of factors, such as a loose connection in the power cord or a faulty switch. To troubleshoot this issue, beginners should first ensure that the power cord is securely plugged into a functioning outlet. If the problem persists, they can check the power cord for any visible damage or fraying and replace it if necessary. Additionally, inspecting the switch for dirt or debris buildup and cleaning it with compressed air or a soft brush may resolve the issue.

Another common issue is the Dremel tool producing excessive noise or vibration during operation. This could indicate a problem with the motor, bearings, or attachment compatibility. Beginners should start by checking that the attachment is securely fastened to the tool and properly balanced. If excessive noise or vibration persists, it may be necessary to inspect the motor brushes for wear and replace them if needed. Cleaning the bearings and applying a small amount of lubricant can also help reduce noise and vibration.

Overheating is another potential issue, especially during prolonged use or when working with demanding materials. If the Dremel tool becomes hot to the touch or emits a burning smell, it is important to immediately turn off the tool and allow it to cool down. To prevent overheating, beginners should avoid pushing the tool beyond its recommended limits and take regular breaks during extended use. Additionally, ensuring adequate ventilation in the workspace can help dissipate heat and prevent overheating.

In some cases, beginners may encounter issues with the Dremel tool's performance, such as reduced speed or power output. This could be due to a clogged air vent, worn motor brushes, or a dirty or damaged collet. Cleaning the air vents with compressed air and inspecting the motor brushes for wear can help restore the tool's performance. If the collet is dirty or damaged, it may need to be cleaned or replaced to ensure proper attachment compatibility and secure tool operation.

Finally, if none of the troubleshooting steps resolve the issue, beginners should contact Dremel customer support or consult the user manual for further assistance. Dremel offers comprehensive support services, including troubleshooting guides, warranty coverage, and repair services, to help beginners address any issues they may encounter with their tools. By staying vigilant and proactive about maintenance troubleshooting, beginners can ensure their Dremel tools remain reliable and efficient tools for years to come.

Advanced Tips and Tricks

Enhancing Precision in Detailed Work

Achieving precision in detailed work with a Dremel tool requires a combination of technique, practice, and the right accessories. For beginners venturing into more intricate projects, mastering these advanced tips and tricks can elevate the quality of their craftsmanship to new heights.

1. **Choose the Right Bit**: Precision begins with selecting the appropriate bit for the task at hand. For fine detailing and intricate cuts, consider using high-speed steel (HSS) or carbide bits, which offer superior durability and control compared to standard bits. Diamond-coated bits are also excellent for precision engraving on hard materials like glass or ceramic.

2. **Adjust Speed Settings**: The speed at which the Dremel tool operates significantly impacts precision. Lower speeds provide better control and are ideal for detailed work, while higher speeds are suitable for rapid material removal. Experiment with different speed settings to find the optimal balance between control and efficiency for your specific project.

3. **Practice Control Techniques**: Developing a steady hand and maintaining consistent pressure are essential for precision work. Practice controlling the Dremel tool with gentle, fluid movements, avoiding jerky or erratic motions that can result in unintended errors. Resting your elbow on a stable surface can also help stabilize your hand for intricate tasks.

4. **Use a Light Touch**: When working on delicate materials or intricate designs, less is often more. Apply light pressure to the Dremel tool, allowing the accessory to glide smoothly over the surface without digging in too deeply. This subtle touch minimizes the risk of accidental damage and ensures precise, controlled cuts and engravings.

5. **Work in Stages:** For complex projects requiring fine detail, break the work into smaller, manageable sections. Work on one section at a time, gradually refining the details before moving on to the next. This approach helps maintain focus and precision, preventing overwhelm and ensuring consistent quality throughout the project.

6. **Employ Guide Aids**: Guide aids such as templates, stencils, or straight edges can assist in achieving precise lines and shapes. Secure the guide aid firmly in place before beginning work, then use it as a reference point to guide the movement of the Dremel tool. This helps maintain alignment and consistency, especially when working on intricate designs or patterns.

7. **Practice Patience**: Precision work often requires patience and attention to detail. Take your time to carefully plan each step of the project, double-checking measurements and alignments before proceeding. Resist the temptation to rush through the process, as haste can lead to costly mistakes that may compromise the final result.

8. **Fine-Tune with Finishing Tools**: After completing the detailed work with the Dremel tool, use fine-grit sandpaper or polishing accessories to refine the surface further. This step smooths out any rough edges or imperfections, enhancing the overall quality and professionalism of the finished piece.

9. **Evaluate and Adjust**: Periodically step back to evaluate your progress and make any necessary adjustments. Assess the symmetry, alignment, and overall aesthetics of the work, making minor tweaks as needed to ensure perfection. Don't hesitate to revisit previous steps or make refinements until you're satisfied with the outcome.

By incorporating these advanced tips and tricks into their practice, beginners can elevate their precision and craftsmanship with the Dremel tool, unlocking new possibilities for intricate detailing and refined finishes in their projects. With patience, practice, and a commitment to continuous improvement, mastering precision work becomes an achievable goal, opening doors to even more ambitious and rewarding creative endeavors.

Speed and Pressure Techniques

Understanding speed and pressure techniques is crucial for harnessing the full potential of a Dremel tool, especially for beginners transitioning into more advanced projects. By mastering these techniques, users can achieve optimal results in terms of precision, control, and efficiency.

Speed control is one of the key features of a Dremel tool. Adjusting the speed settings allows users to tailor the tool's performance to the specific task at hand. For delicate or intricate work, such as engraving fine details or etching delicate materials like glass, lower speeds are preferred. This provides greater control and minimizes the risk of accidentally damaging the workpiece. Conversely, higher speeds are suitable for tasks that require more aggressive material removal, such as cutting through metal or shaping wood. Experimenting with different speed settings on scrap material can help users determine the ideal speed for their particular project.

Pressure techniques also play a significant role in achieving desired outcomes with a Dremel tool. Applying the right amount of pressure can make the difference between smooth, precise cuts and rough, uneven surfaces. When using cutting or carving attachments, it's important to apply consistent, even pressure to ensure a uniform result. Too much pressure can cause the tool to bog down or jump, leading to mistakes or damage to the workpiece. Conversely, too little pressure may result in ineffective cutting or carving. Finding the perfect balance of pressure takes practice and may vary depending on the material being worked on.

In addition to controlling speed and pressure independently, mastering the coordination of both variables is essential for achieving optimal results. For example, when engraving intricate designs on metal, maintaining a steady hand while adjusting the speed to match the intricacy of the design is critical. Similarly, when cutting through thick materials like plastic or fiberglass, applying gradual pressure while adjusting the speed to a higher setting can help maintain control and prevent overheating or melting of the material.

Another advanced technique involves utilizing the oscillation or oscillation-free modes available on certain Dremel models. Oscillation-free mode provides a constant speed regardless of the pressure applied, while oscillation mode automatically adjusts the speed based on the pressure exerted by the user. Understanding when and how to use these modes can further enhance precision and control, particularly for tasks that require varying levels of pressure throughout the process.

Ultimately, mastering speed and pressure techniques requires patience, practice, and a willingness to experiment. Beginners should start by familiarizing themselves with the different speed settings and gradually adjusting their pressure techniques to achieve desired results. As they gain experience and confidence, they can begin to refine their techniques to tackle more complex projects with precision and efficiency, unlocking the full potential of their Dremel tool.

Mixing Mediums and Materials

Mixing mediums and materials is an advanced technique that allows Dremel users to explore new dimensions of creativity and craftsmanship. By combining different materials and mediums, enthusiasts can achieve unique textures, colors, and effects in their projects, elevating their creations to new heights. This advanced tip and trick section will delve into various methods and considerations for effectively mixing mediums and materials with the Dremel tool.

One of the key considerations when mixing mediums and materials is understanding their compatibility. While the Dremel tool is versatile and capable of working with a wide range of materials, some combinations may pose challenges. For example, certain plastics may melt or warp when subjected to high-speed rotary tools, while others may produce harmful fumes. It's essential to research and test different materials before attempting to mix them to ensure compatibility and safety.

Once compatibility is established, enthusiasts can experiment with blending materials to achieve desired effects. For instance, combining wood and resin opens up a world of possibilities for creating unique jewelry, sculptures, or tabletops. The Dremel tool can be used to carve intricate designs into wood before pouring resin to fill the voids, resulting in stunning visual effects.

Similarly, mixing metals such as copper, brass, or aluminum with wood or acrylic can create striking contrasts and textures in jewelry or decorative pieces. The Dremel tool's precision and control make it ideal for engraving intricate patterns or textures onto metal surfaces, adding depth and visual interest to the final product.

Another popular technique is combining different types of stone or glass to create mosaic artwork or jewelry. The Dremel tool equipped with diamond-tipped bits can easily cut, shape, and engrave stone or glass pieces to fit together seamlessly, allowing artisans to unleash their creativity in designing intricate patterns and motifs.

When mixing mediums and materials, it's important to consider the tools and attachments needed for each material. For example, cutting metal may require specialized cutting discs or grinding bits, while engraving glass may necessitate diamond-tipped engraving points. Having a diverse collection of Dremel accessories ensures that enthusiasts have the right tool for every task, enabling them to experiment and create with confidence.

Furthermore, mastering techniques such as layering, inlaying, or embedding allows artisans to create depth and dimension in their projects. For example, embedding metal accents into wood or resin creates eye-catching focal points, while layering different colors of resin produces mesmerizing depth and visual effects.

In conclusion, mixing mediums and materials with the Dremel tool offers endless possibilities for creative expression and experimentation. By understanding material compatibility, exploring different combinations, and mastering advanced techniques, enthusiasts can elevate their craft to new heights, creating one-of-a-kind masterpieces that showcase their ingenuity and passion for craftsmanship.

Expanding Your Skills

Learning from the Community: Resources and Forums

Expanding your skills with a Dremel tool goes beyond the pages of a guidebook; it's about tapping into a vibrant community of enthusiasts, sharing knowledge, and learning from each other's experiences. Online resources and forums serve as invaluable platforms for beginners to connect with seasoned users, exchange tips and tricks, and find inspiration for new projects.

One of the most accessible resources for Dremel enthusiasts is online forums dedicated to DIY projects, crafting, and woodworking. Platforms like Reddit's r/DIY and r/woodworking are bustling hubs of activity, where users share their Dremel projects, seek advice on techniques, and offer guidance to newcomers. These forums provide a wealth of information, from troubleshooting common issues to showcasing innovative uses of the Dremel tool.

Similarly, social media platforms such as Instagram and Pinterest are treasure troves of Dremel inspiration. By following hashtags like #DremelProjects or #DremelCommunity, beginners can discover a myriad of creative endeavors, from intricate wood carvings to stunning metal etchings. Engaging with these communities not only exposes beginners to new techniques but also fosters a sense of camaraderie among fellow enthusiasts.

YouTube is another invaluable resource for visual learners seeking tutorials and demonstrations. Many skilled craftsmen and hobbyists share their expertise through detailed video guides, covering everything from basic techniques to advanced projects. By subscribing to Dremel-focused channels and playlists, beginners can gain insight into different applications of the tool and follow along step-by-step as they refine their skills.

Beyond digital platforms, local maker spaces and DIY workshops offer hands-on opportunities for learning and collaboration. These communal spaces often host classes and events focused on Dremel techniques, providing beginners with the chance to receive personalized instruction, experiment with new attachments, and connect with like-minded individuals in their area.

In addition to online and offline communities, manufacturers and retailers of Dremel products frequently organize workshops and demonstrations. These events offer beginners the chance to interact with Dremel experts, ask questions, and gain practical experience under professional guidance. Whether it's a hardware store workshop or a trade show booth, these events are valuable opportunities for hands-on learning and networking.

As beginners immerse themselves in the Dremel community, they'll discover a wealth of resources and forums waiting to support their journey. From online platforms and social media groups to local maker spaces and workshops, there's no shortage of opportunities to expand skills, seek guidance, and find inspiration. By actively engaging with these communities, beginners can accelerate their learning curve, unlock new creative possibilities, and forge meaningful connections with fellow Dremel enthusiasts.

Taking on More Complex Projects

Once beginners have familiarized themselves with the basic techniques and capabilities of the Dremel tool, they may feel ready to take on more complex projects that push their skills to the next level. While starting small is essential for building confidence, expanding into more intricate and challenging endeavors opens up a world of creativity and possibilities.

One area where beginners can expand their skills is in precision carving and sculpting. While simple carving projects may involve shaping basic designs into wood or soft metals, more complex projects require a deeper understanding of tool control and material properties. Experimenting with different carving attachments and practicing techniques such as relief carving and undercutting can help beginners develop their proficiency in this area.

Another avenue for growth is in the realm of intricate engraving and etching. While beginners may start with basic designs and text, taking on more complex projects involves mastering finer details and achieving greater depth and dimension in their work. By experimenting with different engraving bits, adjusting speeds, and practicing on various materials, beginners can refine their skills and tackle more challenging designs with confidence.

Exploring mixed media projects is another way for beginners to expand their skills with the Dremel tool. Combining materials such as wood, metal, glass, and ceramics opens up endless possibilities for creativity. Whether it's incorporating metal accents into a wooden sculpture, adding texture to a ceramic piece, or embellishing a glass surface with intricate designs, experimenting with mixed media projects allows beginners to push the boundaries of their skills and explore new techniques and aesthetics.

Taking on more complex projects also involves honing problem-solving skills and learning to adapt techniques to suit specific challenges. Whether it's figuring out how to achieve a particular texture or navigating unexpected obstacles during the creative process, beginners can develop their ability to think critically and creatively by tackling projects that push them out of their comfort zone.

Finally, exploring advanced techniques and applications of the Dremel tool can help beginners expand their skills and take on more ambitious projects. From creating three-dimensional sculptures to intricate jewelry designs, there are countless ways to push the limits of what can be achieved with this versatile tool. By continuing to learn and experiment with new techniques, materials, and projects, beginners can unlock their full creative potential and take their skills to new heights.

Taking on more complex projects is a natural progression for beginners looking to expand their skills with the Dremel tool. By pushing themselves to tackle new challenges, experiment with different techniques, and explore new applications, beginners can continue to grow and evolve as artisans, unlocking new levels of creativity and craftsmanship along the way.

Customizing Your Dremel Tool and Accessories

Customizing your Dremel tool and accessories presents an exciting opportunity to tailor your tools to suit your specific needs and preferences. By exploring various customization options, beginners can enhance their Dremel experience, improve efficiency, and unlock new creative possibilities.

One of the most straightforward ways to customize your Dremel tool is by selecting the right attachments and accessories for your projects. With a diverse range of bits, sanding drums, polishing wheels, and cutting discs available, you can assemble a collection that caters to the tasks you most frequently undertake. Investing in high-quality attachments ensures better results and longevity for your tools.

Additionally, modifying the grip of your Dremel tool can significantly improve comfort and control during extended use. Many users find that adding ergonomic grips or rubberized coatings to the tool handle reduces fatigue and enhances precision, especially when working on intricate projects that require steady hands.

For those looking to take customization a step further, consider exploring aftermarket modifications and enhancements. Upgrading the motor or power supply of your Dremel tool can provide increased performance and reliability, allowing you to tackle more demanding projects with ease. However, it's essential to research compatibility and safety considerations before making any modifications to your tool.

Another aspect of customization involves creating custom accessories or adapting existing ones to better suit your needs. For example, crafting custom sanding drums or cutting guides tailored to specific project requirements can improve efficiency and precision. Experimenting with different materials and designs allows you to fine-tune your accessories to achieve optimal results.

Furthermore, integrating your Dremel tool into a dedicated workspace or workstation can streamline your workflow and enhance organization. Designing custom tool holders, storage solutions, and workbenches ensures that your tools and accessories are readily accessible and neatly arranged, minimizing clutter and maximizing efficiency.

Exploring software and firmware modifications for digital Dremel tools opens up a world of possibilities for advanced users interested in programming and automation. Customizing tool settings, creating presets, and even integrating the Dremel tool with other devices or software platforms can enhance functionality and productivity, empowering users to tackle complex projects with confidence.

Customizing your Dremel tool and accessories offers a myriad of benefits for beginners seeking to expand their skills and optimize their workflow. Whether through selecting the right attachments, modifying the tool's ergonomics, or exploring aftermarket enhancements, customization allows users to tailor their tools to their specific needs and preferences. By embracing customization, beginners can enhance their Dremel experience, improve efficiency, and unlock new creative possibilities in their crafting endeavors.

Conclusion

As we draw to a close on our journey through "How to Use a Dremel for Beginners," it's essential to reflect on the valuable knowledge and experiences gained along the way. This book has served as a comprehensive guide, equipping readers with the skills, confidence, and inspiration to embark on their Dremel adventures with enthusiasm and creativity.

Throughout the chapters, we've explored the fundamentals of using a Dremel tool, from understanding its components and safety measures to mastering essential techniques like sanding, cutting, engraving, and polishing. We've delved into project ideas, providing step-by-step instructions and troubleshooting tips to help beginners overcome challenges and achieve satisfying results.

Moreover, we've emphasized the importance of experimentation and practice, encouraging readers to embrace mistakes as learning opportunities and to persist in honing their craft. The Dremel tool is a versatile and adaptable instrument, capable of fulfilling a myriad of creative visions, and with each project completed, readers have expanded their skills and unleashed their imagination.

As we bid farewell to these pages, it's important to remember that learning is a continuous journey. While this book serves as a solid foundation for beginners, there is always more to explore, more techniques to master, and more projects to undertake. We encourage readers to seek out additional resources, connect with fellow enthusiasts, and continue pushing the boundaries of their creativity with their Dremel tool.

In closing, "How to Use a Dremel for Beginners" is more than just a guide; it's a companion, a mentor, and a source of inspiration for those embarking on their crafting journey. Armed with the knowledge and skills imparted within these pages, readers are well-equipped to unleash their creativity, tackle new challenges, and transform their ideas into tangible works of art. So, as you set forth on your Dremel adventures, may your hands be steady, your imagination boundless, and your creations a testament to the power of learning and exploration.

Made in the USA
Columbia, SC
01 December 2024

48063988R00070